introspektd:
the lone languishing for love

Tiffany Rachann

introspektd:
the lone languishing for love
Tiffany Rachann

Imagiread
2022

Copyright ©2018 Tiffany Rachann

All rights reserved. This book or any portion thereof may not be reproduced or used in any manner whatsoever without the express written permission of the publisher except for the use of brief quotations in a book review or scholarly journal.

First Printing: 2018

ISBN 978-0-9850268-3-7 (e-book) ISBN 978-1-7355250-0-6 (print)

Imagiread
11601 Shadow Creek Parkway Suite #111-335
Pearland, Texas 77584

www.imagiread.com

Ordering Information:

Special discounts are available on quantity purchases by corporations, associations, educators, and others. For details, contact the publisher at the above listed address.

U.S. trade bookstores and wholesalers: Please contact Imagiread via email at inquiries@imagiread.com.

insight

There's always been some sort of reference to time in my writing. When sifting through journals, I can always pin where I've mentally been by the way I outline the space in time. I've apparently been traveling from and to, with many a companion. The only thing that is left to wonder is how I believe or believed it to be so.

introspektd: the lone languishing for love is an attempt to identify with what those times truly meant, most especially in those instances where I thought love was what it was, only to discover what it wasn't. My only hope is that it resonates. For throughout these pages are but mere messages, reminders that while stories long to be told, the telling will always long to be just.

introspektd: the languishing for love

Sojourn

running
running away from the state of trying
because trying is consideration for having not to be
losing the race
but finding a path in and around epitome
without a plan
passer by
having a grace that you could never explain
shaped like nectar
outlined by disdain
where the ink dries
is the same place it stains
simply because it can
ever such is water abysmal and deep
whereas it rears with all sides
and it's simply positioning to think
more concerned with the direction
not enough about the bringing
to be brought with the buy in
of when you get there
the war within
destructing yourselves
healing how you care
feel that breeze
withstand

introspektd: the languishing for love

Burn

where at first I knew not where I could withstand
I anointed the space
subtly I moved my hands
moreover
at a practiced pace
became one that welcomed you here
this moment as now
vastly near
slow
steady
flickering voraciously and only in between
the enumeration
of you and me

Sanctuary

I want to run through temples with you

letting mountains sway my feet

moving at the pace of the clouds

eager to meet

the core

of either and or

all of you and all of me

introspektd: the languishing for love

Rhythm

the first time was a surprise
a just alright if you had to say
the second time intentional
a bit bigger in a way
the third time
and a fourth
and times to follow all included words
quickly became my most of all
to which I'd reserved
excessive reverie
and stationary appeal
lined with vigor
in all efforts to steal
whatever I'd originally intended

Stayed

now that you know
everything
will you have the input
the ability
the decorum
to stay
and be my heaven steel

introspektd: the languishing for love

Along

along the way
to where I know not
along the way
where the cool breeze is marred deep inside the plot
a place in fact
heart strings intact
you have so much care
ready and fully arrived
waiting for me there
along the way

Order

I was born aware
wherever that is
or at least that's what I think
whenever I can
sometimes I tune it out and act like everyone else
other times I just wait
however
I can
waiting is hard
tricky even
when I can't wait to be aware I just do whatever I feel
and I convince myself that it's a nearly perfect notion
I've yet to learn the art of practice so that I can practice being here
does this count

introspektd: the languishing for love

Posey

purple and green
long and lean
here then gone
right and wrong
more than less
shortly impressed
she finally got her way
now what

Counter

q: Is that dirt or dye
a: either way, it's original

q: Is this quintessential or in stride
a: either way, it's progress

q: Is this denied or embraced
a: there is no difference

introspektd: the languishing for love

Rant

they screaming
you mad
choosing a side from the lesser
two opportunities you thought you had
you came
saw to immediately trust
anyone that told you they too believed in love
never questioning where they came from
only to find
circumstances not so luxurious like you like
situations seemingly unreal
but you was choosing a side
and you chose to feel
tiny thrill
then wanted an escape when that little became still
you'd had enough
girl they screaming over there
you better go get yo tough

Contest

when you didn't know this
most of all there is made a way with life and that became what
it is to become
outlined miracles inside gentle breezes
simply because
when you didn't know this
the force of all albeit and sunshine had its way with time
showed up bold and had all the pieces
simply because
when you didn't know this
the course of it all with an effervescent tide did its thing inside
reflected a stage and left some engaging not unlike that of past
simply because
ineffable with trends
for you were everything there is
when you didn't know this
the middle
no beginning
no end

introspektd: the languishing for love

Occupy

caught
with a purpose
one that no single
could dare have released
from me
captured
the look and feel that says I AM some way in supreme
one that is not completely known yet
trapped
in such a longing that I don't want to be free
from finally all of you and the most of me
what it is I am detained and now see
is what is known as eventually
of which is
the bounty
pricey

Scaled

the woman I've become
my world is my rhythm and my hunger has a thirst
my everlasting is my everything
my experiences last
dual first
my reign a curse
for the sake of subtlety
influence above all
interactive creativity
all for justice

introspektd: the languishing for love

Drift

it's right here
the place I come to proceed
the place I covet
where I am free to bleed
Here
the place where I allude
the place eye come to see
the place that is protectant from me for me
Here
free
miles of serenades
and melodies stretched wide
exacerbating sensations
long slow strides
seemingly with nowhere to hide

Stock

My calm is necessary
My composure is based
My essence is deeply rooted
in the ducts of my taste
My person is essential
My nature is abided
My power is dually footed
and adorned at the waist
My vision is effervescent
My rise is assured
My posture is statue like
preceding all to be endured
My way is jarring
And my expanse takes care
My circumstances are separate
beyond here or there
I AM TIMELESS

introspektd: the languishing for love

Compass

quiet city
loud with pity
nice and gritty
if ever a such thing were to exist
still like story
beautifully boring
at hopes for the
presence it once winced
mince
break of the day
for the severance of ways
as is it repaid
for all that is lost
go figure

Pulse

Hey sis
How you
Just calling
to say
Thanks
Thanks for
showing me
the ins and outs
of everything
where sometimes
love glares
and other times were despaired
All was for the coming of us as one
for I have established that sisterhood
constitutes the battles unsung but won
mirrored vibration

introspektd: the languishing for love

Diverge

pass
pass
long
long
longing
for the shortcut
the heart knows
the heart knows
measure
whether
endeavor
will come close but only near
every moment rose up here
rights all left
secrets unkempt
pass
pass
passed
another phase
long
longing
for the pathway
that leads design to definition
there the heart finds it own way
to ascension

Invitation

come well here
virtue awaits
a seductive hallucination
taking its place
anxiety is impulsive
know that you might
there is no escape
no way out
or within for that matter
when imparting flight
in lift off shake
turbulence that takes
simple understandings and
of gravity and force them be more
labeled as a bird's-eye view
it is that which is in store
life's procession

introspektd: the languishing for love

Action

most resolutions dare to conform
in the same place
same token barreling a change unreformed
essential to the programming norm
or so some perform
and find
showcasing is much adieu
their performance is willingly renewed
by pleasures in raging
and pain in staging

Enclose

layers of surface on
with space in between
sights unheard
sounds unseen
therein lies the inequity of time
in a simple beat
and a charming rhyme
one that is illusive
one that is confined
headed up a road designed
inaccessible
and yet drenched in appeal
a slickers reel
cuts left and aims right
leaving a pre-packaged sample
beckoning one to continue
two pairings seem ample
for the playwright's feather
whilst together
is embellishment from the end sparing the start
inscribed with the mythical
of therein
heart

introspektd: the languishing for love

Echo

you've believed it's done enough convincing
chiton fencing
shock to the place where life used to be
a storm unheeding
wounds unglazed
chattered by their reality
I wonder if anyone else could possibly
feel this way
not having spoke it to themselves
at least in a whisper
you try to convince me that you love me
it's downright unpersuasive
an obvious abeyance
for wealth
I know now your vice is evidential
in belonging to someone else
where you occasionally sometimes are
but from the place I stand
the air above us
describes just how afar
this one may be
not available to attest
on his own conquest
monologues in disconnect
the spleen from the heart
lost aways and then found

Conversion

on the way to become who you can and most must unreason-
ably be
there will be
an incredibly better than the good in the bad plan unseen
and still
come out and well in large fragments
maintained
with skill
and offer homage and attribute to one's self for the sake
no annihilation
no disdain

introspektd: the languishing for love

Sequence

one desires to be 1
but the others aren't at all as on board
they in fact make ultimate decisions
the kind 1 of one can't implore
like saying
be
doin
carving highs out of lows
acts revealed
impalpable skill
to not say
be
do as all the others seemingly suppose
scathed to borderline
inland
transparency waved
as only half's behave
all part of collective plans
until one
day just wants to be more
a meeting
a greeting
an affirmation
the score

Ideal

whereas you are so much to be with
in exchange for such a small expense
my meditation
my association
my recompense
heaven's sequence
having a way with what is in
around the creekside near folds where streams set sail and begin
abound
amend
I consider you a friend
with hands that shape elixir like sun-dried clay
bright colors
euphoric smells
sights that douce iniquities by day
for when I am with you are so much to be with
whereas first place skips a beat accompanied by never to be
I am remiss
pick one

introspektd: the languishing for love

Alone

as in a star in a state that is distant from its own
incumbent insufficient and rightfully unknown
placid by all things and nothing
suggest many seedlings overgrown
setting a tone
and with a substantial hone
in on what the mind has transcribed as reality
forsaken
shaken
riddled for transparency
by walls built stronger than still moments can bear
the place where truth is born
incommensurate
beyond compare

Query: A dedication to Dr. Maya Angelou

why
because you are A daughter
and daughters are the brightness of the sun
amplified
personified
dignified
and then some
your weeping doesn't go unheard or unseen
it's very pitch is the movement
it's force for all things in between
sometimes the last
always the beginning
heaven quarantined
with
yellow, blue and green
too bouts of red, orange, purple and indigo
All equivalent to your soul glow
ahead on the road
I wanna know
if you know who you are
and the supposed capabilities of your hands
goodness is your answer
now take an innerstand

introspektd: the languishing for love

Converter

everything once
has and will in fact happen again
delivery instructed via enemy
via friend
mole in a mountain on end
where the forsaken takes place
wherewithal begins
such a send
off
and
leads
over
to the tiny box in the corner
notes inside forward still
all that remains
are past tense thrills
an evocative death
adorned by an astute overcoming if you will
everything once has in fact happened again
in fabric woven in time stakes eventual
made amends

Testimony

Is this thing on
tap tap
oscillation as solution
purportedly
able to transform
able to spawn
only what
it seemingly
or approximately can
momentary left hand
will it see
that up and coming
is left still yet to be
Is this thing on
Can anybody hear me
Been bewildered long enough
Feeling keen
excitably mean
let's now sing
The most vocal praises
from afar
the going and the coming
a tap dance in my heart
is
this
thing
on

introspektd: the languishing for love

Draft

sold
to the high bidder
the one that forged a start
closely resembling the antiquity in part
laid square in the middle of the beard
it tried to frame
a saddened poise
drained

Mettle

gushing out
unable to maintain
enamored short takes
become harder to retain
the tabard doubles over in pain
instead of the garment that once was worn
in
this
way
partly clever under blue skies
slipped up and gilded with ease
lack of uncertainty
and with not a one to please
so appease
then became one that was adopted near the part
bled to life with reality in exchange
she then offered her heart
for where she was led to the circumference in channel
all frequencies eventually attuned and allegiance upheaval
there today is a blame no more

introspektd: the languishing for love

Request

unfortunate it is
as more often than none
we acquaint some others
with an expectation in sum
once we confirm they are without
a disappointment grows within
and no longer
no longer on second
do we desire to unfriend
so we search and seek
for another to betray
uplifting random strangers
in passing on the way
while said relationships
commiserate inequitable pay

Succession

life force is encapsulating
raw in form
definitively excavating
enveloping
all of the loose change down below
up in baskets offered in exchange for forever more
left-sided by hand yet centered with no number
appears a door
that one is free to wander toward
with the price of tarry
loads of suspense
loads of wonder
are light enough
here
to carry
marry the quest that reveals itself compatible
that has impression enough to conjugate by mating
while knowing that life force in itself is yielding
far beyond encapsulating

introspektd: the languishing for love

State

wish I had some hands that could rewrite that time
the ones I have only hold the whine
of those things that died
on a vine
loud enough for neighbors to hear
a startling trajectory
furthest from near
you are once again
staying up all night to avoid the pain
of laying next to me
pity in the middle
how when and where did such between us dwindle
last CD on the spindle
has recorded muffled and moans
done got so used to co-sleeping with our son that sex don't make   me   feel   so   grown
yet disowned
the last 4 years
did that for certain ones that asked
those were the ones who never knew a flask
of tears existed in tote and over the phone outside of hours on end
my lamenting
took to descend
dead now
all gone
it's been 6 months since we separated
this last month was when life opened up and illustrated a presence having shone
on me and so back to have to begin
thought about you after all and how you were actually a good friend

despite my impending
personal demise
emotions still rise
and I wanna call you and say
I miss you
come home love
today

introspektd: the languishing for love

Repose

lost it
too busy trying to hold on
it eventually bantered in the besought launch of long hours
cleverly passed
it's gone
hopeful for a return this time
to a place separate from solar temperament but in the quiet of
the breeze-like balm, alas
every morning
every night
something different
ever bright
righteously sanctioned by the evergreen's touch
having lost a gross majority seemingly equates as modesty
in fact
I haven't lost much

Ramble

but
that
is
not
what
was
said

introspektd: the languishing for love

Command

but
can I be in love with you solely as me
twin flame
unadulterated
saturated
adorned
free
the whispering willow knows a query we do not
and a loose leaf by the creek plays jester for jot
TING
they all recognize the lot
signature attained
improvisational remains
a such way
a such place
heaven's rigor mortis
can I be in love with you on the sole of today
meta sane
predicated
during seasons beyond
taking on this circumstance
as the reunion
retorted
finally healed
swayed
a rising up of heartbeats
in the burning bed
lay
as much and many as sure is
my answer

introspektd: the languishing for love

Admit

catching anything
everything
claiming it all as mine
trajectory stagnated
wind blowing opposite the chime
loose change
a dime
or so it sometimes seems
moving about
around
seance is time
an abscission performed
by the latter-day of indoctrination
the same white coat
loose change
the amount con

Actuate

bowed over by extraction
streaming
pouring
spilling out
stationary
with eminence as the tailor
the coil of the universe
has designed and is seconds into with being complete
synchronicity
as the introduction to being
everlasting and fated
where an eternal increase shall part
still bowed over by extraction
tears flowing
I offer my heart

introspektd: the languishing for love

Originale

the best thing she could have done was be an example of those things alive
it offered me a vantage point
illustrated my desire to thrive
quite and frank both knew she never tried
happenstance has it and it would have been better to have died
so it did
undenied
paternity confirmed hers with wombs that carried other babies
with pitches only those called could hear
redefined
such infancy in tote and in turn created a what is known as a healthy fear
fear of knowing
fear of sinking
fear of being just in
so much so that tears drudge abundantly as there no recourse for such sacred sins
the best thing she could have done is what she did not
wrote my beginning she did but only I can master my plot
cheers to my mama

Posture

resolve
evolve
all with direction on no end
the epitome is welcomed but never befriend
dead on arrival or as common can seem to stall
a case
even oddly enough has proved itself coming with dawn
clavier
salve sayer
mornings in gong
melody minus song
where all of this muster in decision comes from
garner pride
take stance
you really are

introspektd: the languishing for love

Proxy

prescriptive
preemptive
fallacies where brute like convictions used to tarry
horizon maimed asunder
understanding nothing with one more to carry
makeshift math
modern by late days tale
proof of certainty
arts of science
man's boldest bias
system fail
quantitative

Entrance

all of my covering is on the floor
somehow separated
parted at the door
all that was cantered beckons to bequeath more
of the perimeters of you
most especially those I most adore
our majesty
so much so that there no need to culminate
what's left to be explored
all things unending seemingly parted at the door

introspektd: the languishing for love

Apologue

text
reply
where alas there should be some echo of reverence
some point of preference where we are regarded
open-hearted
and not ashamed as I thought I would find myself to be
there is the long withstanding
short and out fielded
tallying up as feelings between you and me
I shouldn't want to speak to you
I shouldn't want to feel your words drape above mimicking
the order of a smile only envisioned perfectly still
I shouldn't have these desires
the ones that offer my accordance
for it you and your will
in exchange
rearrange
the depths of my golden
yet newly lone heart
adjust the frequency
located inertia
stagnate all over in start
to allow whatever will happen supplementing what ever shall in fact be
tallying up these feelings
my imagination where there literally lives you and me

introspektd: the languishing for love

Case

You
don't
love
me
the
way
you
said
you
could

Partition

hear comes the particle
set and coarse in a way that makes force
movement
hear comes the influence that forces boards to be
rigid and staunch
sound
hear meets the conjugate
appending with signatures of all involved
activity
designated and finally approved

introspektd: the languishing for love

Commonplace

I put those shrivels and whimpers in the jar that used to sit on the sill that owned all of the day's possibilities and often admired by tomorrow's multitude
in the cupboard
behind the old broken plates and cups and bowls
that used to stand tall to serve
but now cannot
so that the pieces of each could congregate and meet
perhaps introducing a side that doesn't seem so much in despair
for the reason for wishing them to be well is simply because I am hopeful that they will learn
someone still cares

Commute

it's gone
that same hallowed and most likely to be stagnant err that has
kept me in bankrupt company all of these years
or is it

it's arrived
that same emulsive grief that has a tide lawless enough to
sweep ones life expectancy down into a murky and absolved
abyss
or has it

it's passing
that same instinctive mode of torture that forms a resolve only
to reveal its keen and ridiculous circumstantial nature
or is it

now here
right now
mostly condemned

introspektd: the languishing for love

Overhead

by far the most expensive
house is that one deeded intuition
should by far be the most obvious in kind
at the corner of nixed and fruition
forging a path where the participants make way to compromise
lies
where actors who are great pretenders
change lines and have altered endings
parted in half on stage are their children
and this seemingly goes on for days
sponsored in part by and made possible in fact by
a common currency
a disheveled wage
rage

Handle

the small of the tea cup
made for green jasmine
has the same carry of flow
as the funnel that transports oil
susceptible
short lived
pronounced
the grasp on the long spoon
made for mixing
is the same type of gather
as the awning closer than near but across the way
glaring
dense
reverted
the letters written
on the back of the receipt
have the same meaning that the words unspoken
here and now are encased
straddling
approximated
particular
onward wonder up for grabs

introspektd: the languishing for love

A Midst (Solar Return)

underneath the during
where while watches me sleeping standing still
a moment unravels
and interjects its skill
steadfast
determined
fixated for soothing
layers of evermore
placid and moving
currently towards magnificence
a whathaveyou if you will
yesterday's laden has officially become tomorrow's thrill
it's a blessing to be here 37 years to the day
my only prayer is for many more moments where I am determined as if
in the same way

Copious

the rambling fumble

moves through the room

pacing

searching

trying

the rambling fumble

gives up

calls chair over

facing

tears

with hands held high

joined in stillness

introspektd: the languishing for love

Tall order

untangle

here

now

Here

You are

Rhetoric

what do I believe
what do I believe
meaning has humanity reached a place where its condition
precedes it
or what did you mean on that last Facebook post when you
said that the time has forth come for us to learn
you know so tell me which one
because either way I'll have to consecutively define
the line
that will come to bear cross herein and possibly separate us
once again
identify the question
my friend
identify the question
as if your intention was to discover the absolute
as in one of those who knows
that either way
either one
marks a place
having an identical face
of ones who inquire as so
as soon as I get a firm grip on what I believe
trust me when I say
you'll be the second to know

introspektd: the languishing for love

Wind

brush
    meander
            cross the line
of what just two seconds before and ago
seemed along with sublime
crossed the line
on all my divine
whisper
halter
redefine what's dear
because what I thought of five ago
couldn't have drawn you near
redefined what's dear
return what's mine
for all my divine
ode to the tempest of change

Range

eloquence
the foremost hence
indulging a press that has never before had a form
where effortless
are incredulous
are combined to evade those things once considered norm
in unparalleled sight
an unending flight
the place where bounty is set only on dear hearts
a measure enlist
a sensational twist
forever more and then some kept for none
gaze meets accordance
all that is here is undone
free to be

introspektd: the languishing for love

Grail

stone
wash
blackened
harsh
cording barred by the cracks in enclosure met
plaster
time
makeshift
mine
rippled against and shattered
crashing beget
when all seems obvious and as if things are bound to a way
the elements shift slightly and on moves the day
plan your escape
for winds of change blow steadily and do mostly unequipped
the very thing you say you hope for comes in
life's constant drip

Guise

a certainty of measure
stocked full with variety supposed
unclaimed
the right way
comes and adjusts
the chains
there is a tendency to control what believes itself to be sane
growing wilder
untilled
destined to not be tamed
never the exact way
still forces and shifts
a square remains
there is a stage to mull over where props cannot be changed
always
setting atmosphere
settling of hemisphere
a certainty of measure
for all weeds that harrow near

introspektd: the languishing for love

Recount

as if it were
as if it were to be
as if it were to be entirely
roadside
in need of assistance to appease
my side of the story is as follows
it was way too much to deal with
way too much to see
I'd like to think a sensual perception
love's perception of me

Diluted

a stillborn tear that trickles down on the face of one
meets the flesh of the garner in a city named Conundrum
where all those that visit leave with a map of sum
other place not yet here
a churned observation moves up the road and across mighty
terrain
stops cold to assume the placid effect of the moments reign
something is coming, there is no need to explain
to another place not yet here
a reconciliation
offering up of an extraction that only few are able to note
the stiffness of the the little piece of paper
the unravel of its smote beckons
for what is not
incredibly is and in that place tied to everywhere shall live
an explorer of said domain
for those who have never known him he goes by Maraud
his assigned name

introspektd: the languishing for love

Inheritance

Be big enough to admit
after all it gets you in
Be bold enough to answer
after all it is only your call
Be glad enough
Be great enough
Be wise enough to know that after is all

Inclusive

the wandering of an answer
meets the shaping of a quandary
where combination nears slate like condition
made especially for the laundry
the most expensive tawdry
now bearing disgrace
shining down as agitation
the gathering now common place
the same at the foot as does with the head
oscillate the addling
dance with the rhythm that is presiding instead
now add tread
and go forward to the answers within

introspektd: the languishing for love

Visage

early rise
late slumber
all that is to be seen in between shall be
enterprise
demise asunder
where as it lands
marks without stain
recognized
clean
waves deterred
vibrancy haltered
envoy vetted
with an open course of wild stemmed dreams
midday resonance
with eves of clairvoyance
enamored as in
all that is to be seen in between shall be

Dye

yellow and then black
stars are in that order
a still therein with no lack
transference
surrounded by occurrence
citing its very own evolution as those that amount
have plenty
new city
new state
new calibration
clean slate
stars are black as night but still manage a brilliance
stars make up cellular construction as
I AM

introspektd: the languishing for love

Opulence

raise
so much so that a dance is noticed in one's reflection of a sky
income accessible
at the rate that past spending could not match nor square for-
ward
wearing a chroma now to illuminate toward
a similar ritual in one's own infested eye
plain and ordinary
lacking yet customary
novice
the best place for exchange
best place for circumstance
a pardon of feaze
welcomed at first glance
raise
so much so that a rhythm assumes all sides with the cracks in
the walls
no floors
no ceilings
no cubicles
no stalls
returning to a cultivated interest
issued by life's uninhibited romance
raise
the skies have opened

Praise

I
didn't
expect
as
much

introspektd: the languishing for love

Turn it up (level)

no idea
not one that ever said that I could catch this much
not one even with many that could compare to finality's touch
this was abrupt
but steel feeling unparalleled while positioned for me to maintain
"she performing a query, her pitch promises to be insane"
I heard the organizer whisper
had this been orchestrated
had it been contemplated
considered by those powers that enormously are to be
if it had I was uncertain
one would think they would have informed me
substantial glee
the stage
those lights
unable to stare out
without regard to might
so elevated played on
drew the energy inside
but after what seemed prolonged seconds
no other place was there to hide
I was snapping fingers and moving about
had a rhythm inside so mighty that it chose to permeate out
had never been privy to such beat
had never lined up said ego to such a feat
from where I rest right now
a steady seat
beat as if worn
beat like scorn
beat in such a way
that I introduced myself to a new scale of say

kept beating
fears clutched and seating for only those who wanted a place in awe
my time had finally come and suddenly greatness of destiny now didn't seem so far
who is another to tell me I know not a star
how par
take for this course that I have immediately chosen
there is no ramification greater than this door to never have closed and
I will use the time that follows to celebrate this as success
pad and paper
curtains draped inward as the director calls NEXT
up to bat
today's catch
a degree

introspektd: the languishing for love

Another Ramble

but
that
is
not
what
was
said

44 days

no thumbs up
no new followers
no talk of any sorts in the last 44 days
what brings me here
what separates me in this place from all of the other there is in this world at only here
what can do such a thing
I realize that in trying to figure what it is that I am doing here that I have somehow sent signals out for more than just direction but also in patience in a vector like pose and a soft waters to help me enjoy the heat of it all when the stragglers begin arriving.
the help has arrived
I know so
I feel it to be
and I accept it as it is
it's been 44 days since I have come here and sought my parking be validated by this establishment that I so proudly own.
44 days of blessings. 44 days of all that life can give.
I bow

introspektd: the languishing for love

Y-ide eye

eye
eye write word with lower casing impending their own self-imposed growth
growth
eye write my word with growth impending that they will in-turn and fertilize
fertilize
eye write my word from fertilizer because I know their glory seeks impending fertile grounds
grounds
eye write my word
eye write on my own grounds

To You

Thank you for reading this far. Thank you for being here with me.

introspektd: the languishing for love

Again

feeling around in the dark
I move my hand swift against the light
sight
beyond
any that would ever be conjured
congregated in sail or fellowship
I met you
present Captain
present Quartermaster
present crew for opposition that took all following commands
next time

Cache

said trance
and those nights that I am blank inside allow the day's
happenstance to pen my hide away
from this travesty when I'd conform
to be normal marked by many day
if ever there was a thing
ever a thing
ever several beings
they'd all be arsenal's absent poise
surefire is certainly more like
a muster nearer to fertile seed sends for others' on this hike
the mountain top
alas wonder
alas sovereignty
alas whom I am designed to be
for it is in those nights that I am blank inside where I'd bid grace
for it's stock-heavy store
to come upon and make me over to what deems towards forever more
here I live
still

introspektd: the languishing for love

Blame

an adopted existence
the place where foster lacks care
that has a medium degree
everlasting of anyone
of two or three there
utter despair
who goes there
those who seek the belonging of free will
over another those who are intimidated by the still
in waters that run
rise high and eventually meet the mountains in streams
because in those strides lie therein the answer of one
two
three's being
who signs up for the class ready to take on its full core
when notified of its requirement

Debtor

it feels as if an apology is due
it looks as if the grantee should be you
but before i bid adieu
and pause this scene
allow me explanation
allow me in between
this jury
this judge
this episode
all an act
was designed to face you but somehow landed you're back
I can admit at this point that there was an exclusive prevalence
that abhorred anything relating to our relevance
fuck, it.
I'm selfish already
just needed you to fill the glass
so I could set it down easy and watch others walk past
to the storefront of my adulation
the place where I could again barter
without care for your feelings
without care for your obvious honor
it's no wonder this world I reside in leaves me unclothed
naked with intention
resulting in greed robe
betrothed

introspektd: the languishing for love

The Count

one half-dozen and a short run with time
continues to keep you on my mind
in places where 13 stays in constant as does the summer
boil down, heat trotted, welcome the new comer
fall, fall, bow down at nearing a quarter pass
almost with new seasons, yet already forgotten the one past
I lose count when I am active
I lose count when I am bored
I lost count in search of
keeping count for what is evermore
just cross that out and carry the line that serves 2.
no cents made of now, no sense made of you

Signed,
The Scorekeeper

Be-wholed

the days of half-loving
and being half-loved are over
they've come forward in finality and have moved on to another
I wonder who she is
I wonder how she now gives
will it be me in the same manner
will it be me in size and weight maybe statue
or will she be taller
will she unintentionally free
illustriousness in damning thoughts
as her only intention bunking distraught
will she be just like me
more in the sense of me in the past
me in the measure of downward cast-
ed to a place that had always been
without comfort to my very soul
will she be like me instead old
her style her grace
hidden behind grief's face
however shall she most exist
how I wish I could meet her on her road and seal her fate
with an otherwise kiss

introspektd: the languishing for love

Comfortable

come for the table
that has been prepared in sync
its adorning is aesthetic yet its mission obsolete
come for the table
that has been equipped with a crew
its selection unending and its variety shown as anew
come for the table
this place where celebrants meet easy
to discuss their inability and to scoff down all things pleasing
come for the table
where its dressing with fat happiness awaits the inside of you
its perversion a barter as your life its bid ado
an empty chair

_____
_____

And I quote

"It is my ability to respond to the processes of growth.
With that, it becomes my willingness to create additional channels to help me track it all.
Subconsciousness reigns supreme."

introspektd: the languishing for love

Environ-meant

open air
open state
continual thought
continual pace
our near first encounter similar to this number of the same
never an experience like today
wet
dry
illicit
high
bound for moments meaning more
I've finally learned to let you lead
timely new management for what is in store
I've always adored
my nose in the fold of your neck
as my top lip meets your pulse
all that surrounds us now
is perfections' curse
anomaly

The Director's Cut

it seemed be the point and place commensurate yet unsuspected
it seemed be the time and space approximately detected
towards the truth of what we believed, our connected
there came forward a movement
evidence shows editing where placement is regarded
set appeared rearranged
as fast as we reconnected
released and then prayed for new beginnings
was as fast as the divine intercepted with its own tale of ending
I had believed it to be a love
I had known it to have magnitude
but after reading the screenplay in its entirety
my certainty is a change in attitude
action

introspektd: the languishing for love

Profound

found after the fact
the presence of wonder is excelled by the process to clarify
multiple things as absolute
the progress therein is seemed tumultuous but then offers
one-siders for resolute
by then
all prior dealings become those that contemplation remembers
very well
a brewing of necessity at the melody pace of shrill
certainty becomes the measure where seeping holes are
sealed
found after the fact
the ever-knowing essence of what an answer truly is
tone offered up by many questions and the lives of each singular one lived
all happenstance
one level up
move to that place

Attraction

mostly parted pathways that scant in representation
mirrored as reality with accordance to the beholders' adaptation
brought forth by chambers that house cognition that kills
and bury the said victim in the living cemetery still
that was then
the same mostly parted pathway is dueled and with now clairvoyance prime
has rendered new construction of the preceptors mind
bringing forth masonry that houses order of one's entire will
and awakens all possibilities of a novel life still
allure

introspektd: the languishing for love

Desire

second in command patiently waiting to become first
its reign is one of presence
most considerable in worth
in all accordance
whereby impetuous
nonetheless nature still
no abhorrence
all perseverance lest its continuity is predicated solely on thrill
but by zeal
by pleasurable peace
by fabrics unprepared
this reality takes place where brilliance lives unmeasured
my very own countess of manifestation
said desire resides by my own ruling class
the birth of a nation

Commission

an accompanied mission one that is placed for the appease
of all things joined and circumstantial are in fact all things soon
to be freed
a go with where the journey itself has an indifferent pace
a come to where each stop doubles as a purposed face
a palace
a shrine
a castle where the unbridled come to merry
who so ever should join me on this road be reminded in their
own fairy
their own magic
their own determination
their own accordance wherever and however that may be
the preparation alone for this assignment is atonement for self
candidacy
the addition

introspektd: the languishing for love

And I quote

"I still don't know that clarity has an exact price. I think instead that it is best valued at the preceptors allowance."

Medium

what liquid
what picture
what verse shall it be
to remove me from this reality
and admit me to effervescence
I shall pick the one or several that I find fitting
and that affords the most
the ones that vindicate duplicity in self and bring forth great
philosopher's ghosts'
what herb
what melody
what place shall I go
to settle me in balance
where only what is reaped is allowed sewn
now serving
small

introspektd: the languishing for love

Libations

package undone but laced with completion
not a gift by far but a testament of discretion
the secret
my secret
our secret all in our own
the same secret that has incessantly anointed its perform-
ance----with the counterpart being that comes to fruition as otherwise
an unnerving arthritis with knees unable to meet the demand of the climb
this is more evident than reality and more prudent than all in order belief in between
this is the most obvious of gifts as its all that is to ever seem drunkenness

Picture This

there are several knocks at the door
each one with a different tone but rapped harder than the one before
once answered the begging assumes
a combination begins
collectively entertaining me
color-full new friends
the first is a sonnet
the next is just one line
the third
two words describing
more advanced than styles behind
the categorizing of thoughts justified and about
they've come today because they were dying to get out
and shred that illuminated marquee
prohibiting in all of these corners
a new welcome is due
the dawning of creative quarters
welcome home

introspektd: the languishing for love

Glistens

a sparkle
a trance
the branding is new every time
a beginning
an end
spectacular is utmost and entwined
sight beyond sight
all is simple and atoned
uplifted in stance
by beauty it's full grown
the reflection therein
is the same one out with
it's the majesty of circumstance
the divine's first and only kiss
hear by photo-reception
embrace it
partitioned

Hue

the gray outline
and the recollection of the fright
remind me that the solitude is here again
and its form is labeled spite
the smoky haze that fills squealing pipes on their way to extinguish fate
remind me of the realistic compounding of church versus your state
the twinkle that glows from over yonder where that post has a base attached
will be the only figure that remains for those who choose to speculate to view
the passing away
the coming forth all for the brand of new
the gray outline is permeated and dense by its respect
an outline all the same
superior in quality and utmost in all concepts

introspektd: the languishing for love

Confusion

I am working again
on my relationship with the pen
and for whatever reason out of the best of blue
here alone enters you
your bags are at the door
it appears you've come to stay
there is a single dote
and you assume its place
I stand up to greet you and find slow stillness in my pace
so very hard to believe I've remembered every detail of your face
your arms
your sweat
your essence
all of your divine creativity
you were always good at picking fine time and today is no exception so I see
what is it I must say to you to release you from my dreams
what is it I must do with myself to recreate things as they seem
what is it I must find and bare down on to stop loving you as I do
what is it I ask as I have asked before
what is left to prove
we both know I capture you whenever south winds come my way
we both know I long for your inequities when you are the furthest away

you and that place in my mind we go to leaves me incredibly
raw and perpetually sore
as in the past I ask today that you not come by anymore
you are the reason I don't love him and I could never be
in the place where blossoms quince all of life's possibilities
you are the reason I appoint somber when otherwise introspection says all is well
you are the one who has in fact damned me to my own isolation in this hell
I was with you was with you was with you when you left me with now
I was with you and then not and I have yet to figure how
it's hard to ask and horrible to wish such a beauty from above
I've denied you before but now I cannot
please come well as often as you please beloved
my addling for you is inside

introspektd: the languishing for love

Impressed

they say it's like a blog
the place where pressing thoughts are displayed and cataloged
for whomever is shopping for such on that particular day
depending on their purchase they too go away feeling the same way
that the messenger did when they decided to lay such words flat-
lining is the way and emergent is the stat
impressed we are
more-so
grateful
for
written
word

E-motion

there's a signature on the glass that sees fit to be one's will
tis the same marking that normally represents a still-
ness of evolution as we fascinate ourselves to another state
swiftly flowing but relentless at a calculated pace
you ain't been nowhere no one else can't go
you ain't built no such incubator
that their science allows you to grow
a microscopic like organism that is fully equipped with its own map
with a constellation that convinces modern users that there is time in form of steps
the closest thing to revolution in every single form
reminds me of a brand new picture frame that outlines a photo
that has been worn then torn
it's world wide all-right

introspektd: the languishing for love

Please

where is that cat of yours
the one you sometimes keep on a leash
the one that has a carnivorous roar at the same time is a feast
you know the one that you let roam from time to time without purpose nor plan
the one you invite to purr as overflow because only it can
the cat that lives to escape and sneak up on a party uninvited
that dam cat
always in some shit leaving many a home ignited
with all kinds of turmoil because it knows no more than what it actually wishes
led astray by many a day with undefined persistence
where is that cat of yours
the one you to better quickly tame
the one you need to learn how not to rent because owning is the name of this game
don't sell yourself

Friends

met an amazing chica just the other day
she was fierce and poised in a most glorious way
her shine and candor always spoke on her behalf
and when she opened her mouth it was obvious that her gift wasn't gab
but action! take one or two or three even to learn from this chick here
the superior melody she owned pierced every single ear
regardless if it was desired she did so with a stride
it clearly didn't take long for me to decide
to befriend her and care for her and I would myself with my own
In the short time I have known her our reverence has deepened, my how I've grown
Her name is Faith

introspektd: the languishing for love

Abound

still waters reflect the channeling of dexterity
flowing waters reflect the accordance of prosperity
both assume the position welcoming the onlookers glance
which is as harmonically abridged for choosing their own dance
unscathed yet neutral powerful even in one place
yet incredible and forceful having ability to change
any one things face
a composition for water is a tremendous resign
the fullness of address offered in sole by the divine
keep growing

Remove

there is a development of sorts that is made for receiving
that is cleverly masked by fear and deceiving
I say your name
to go from a time and start out towards another
is to wane variety and perplex down under
I call it insane
to try and order something that is clear and congruent
but so without cause
while acknowledging deep breaths we have explained are for pause-
ing here because I know that if we go on still
that most things we have taken away
we have also consciously killed
take it away

introspektd: the languishing for love

Platform

there is an elegance of the pen that overwhelms all others
a formation of propriety that no one can put asunder
grand and outreaching as wide as it is
essential to the soul because it freely gives
what a win
it commences as the shape of what's revealed and has become
the aptitude of one's attitude leaving no points of reference undone
there is an elegance of the pen that is one that shares with delight
a solidified adaptation that duals as the very transverse that fuels the night

Capture

when I write

I am doing so to you

to offer a response for all that you do

it is my way of everlasting as set forth in your promises

it is my way of connection as done in your kiss

it is the bliss in accordance of all that shall be

It is my humility in expression for these gifts received

introspektd: the languishing for love

Scenery

the richest in ivy
the most harmonic in scheme
the landscape of all time
eventual in scene
that which is a color as used for inheritance
the same color as foundation for flowers when they dance
where shall riches of all most highness go
yes to the magic of this hue that has been carefully bestowed

A Wake

narrowed pathway led by the smell of flowers
adorned by visitors near and far
open doorway inviting all to an exclusivity in presence above
the stars
tears of many greet most in sounds of symphony
the understanding is not there
they think I am leaving
instead
Eye've come to stay in a sacred being of the divine
those same flowers bless my existence into sublime
an infinite path as oppose to ceremonial decline
intervention by peace as traded for in pyramids of time
I've arrived

introspektd: the languishing for love

Sent-I-meant

keeping mine heart away from yours has been an unknown bare
the still of knowing
the thrill of flowing is absent and without compare
where could it be now that I must find it to share
that fashioned love of more than one that gives the moon its glare
a thunderous heart sends telegram of everything natural as it is to be
I wish no more to do the chore of keeping your love away from me

Disgrace

who knowingly closes doors on humility
who shall live in days where they never see her face
complaining on end where beginnings would normally be
holding magnificence captive for none other to ever place
wasting and soiled by gluten and fear
with a reptilian slithering like pattern
what we yearn for is always near
meanwhile we resort to things not mattering

who knowingly bears down doors on grace
those who have never dreamt of seeing her beautiful face
she can never die

introspektd: the languishing for love

Station

wavelength
as short as the newest pattern of my hair
not crass, not particular by any means but just there
feeding from the energy that tosses through and about
travels are a delight and seemingly stout
no drought
just flow and ebb
sometimes reverse and not in order
this station is one of definite barter
Frequency

Expectation

surely requesting such has impressed a bit of the unknown
unwavering thoughts force me to carry them as my own
frayed
recanting statements of being amidst of past state
dismayed
I am alone in requesting such of an impression that I know that you have not
where it is not normally advised I shall impend and make it forgotten divided by itself remains magical in one

introspektd: the languishing for love

Webbed

the room has divided
one part absence the other presence
all the while there is no sense in it at all
a change in currency with most of never mind
for those to take use
look for the new general to take base
and tax the poor for their hind-
sight is never what it thinks it should be
reality of facade
yet the new system believes we are free

Objectified

mostly apparent in the way you glance
you are carefully crafting your words
apparent and growing towards a stare
that leaves a screech that only mine ear heard
you are considering the inconsiderable
outwardly diminishing
my value as a womb-man
to less than that of cut throats
ages and places where
right here
repression becomes reality

introspektd: the languishing for love

Land-guage

tone down the speaking
and up the radar
because here in the driest of lands
you won't make it very far
if all you can bring is sound from mouths
instead of a sense of nature's rhythm
pandemonium posing as hydration is where one will surely drown

Plank

undefined yet refined
one is indeed entitled to a glory that is all but seen
subjective and permeated
emergent in height and weightlessly thin but absorbed as a sheen
no one or two greater than of when and must
where life grabs hold and won't expel is the normally the point of attesting purpose

introspektd: the languishing for love

Condense

without fear nor fame of tales or blister of a scheme
there is sit and wonder
where time seems to be adjusting in mill
with all purpose
most in definition and yet some imagination
there is what is spat and put asunder
the ideal that every wave eventually meets a hill
a prayer of sorts
and meditation of the helpless but full in sight of this world
she continues to introduce her pattern
where lines meet swirl

Third class

plane
blank slate or method by which I take flight
either the aura's they both beckon cite beyond sight
train
rapid movement or luster of obedience
either predicament and every which way is a definite right
traveling has gotten me this far
with unmeasurable validity
the height of all super in the stars
to the place where I land me

introspektd: the languishing for love

Weather or not

I write despite
I around its bound
I prove certainties move
that happens in me when i hear "it" coming from afar
I ignite the process
I resolve the distress
I play captive to its tress
as if it were my only star
if i couldn't write
no placement shall be
no seasonal process
simply no veritable me

_____

_____

Other Rambling

is
that
what
you
heard

introspektd: the languishing for love

Cease and desist

a moment
stricken at :02
how will it mean
how shall it go
same way it came
quietly
bringing no captives
except ones that enslaved themselves to be
a moment
pivoting change
most like perilous
brimming with native
those who know why they come from
I say to the moment "you are invited but I have no welcome"
the moment says to me "you have now been baptized, be strongest in my forearm"
direct
shuns
a fierce coastal storm brewing in the bay
a lovers' old flame allowing memory for its way
a piece of paper designed by what can
the brokenness remaining from what used to be a (womb)man
loose change
strong will
albeit all of the matter in between
is the exact push the same in pull meets and offers up what we know as life's plea
succession

introspektd: the languishing for love

Aristocrat

there is a chirp that echoes sweeter
an order of epoch that seems neater
when the pouring down is suddenly ceased
illumination
a wave that offers contentment
a voice that is seemingly shorter of resentment
when the vapors rise up as they may
undetermined
at the place of passing, all elements meet one time
albeit they are forced to change the owners' mine
and seek individual progression within
Salute! Stand Down Wise Ones
and shalt recognize by their existence that they have already
been set to settling in and win

Germinate

The ants are crowded about
the tail of the worm's smudge
in deep conversation
about parts to be lugged
for burial or infestation
they are livid for their place
dutiful response to such a decision occupies their today
Nature is discerning
for the sake of its own good
since I strive for the state as well
maybe I too should

introspektd: the languishing for love

Opening Night

remote
find the channel that directs the very beat of my heart
whispering shadows
still brightness that lives only when parts
played by only the two of us and encore is needed once but more
you are an abysmal delight that seeks the comfort of mine own pores
be easy with our display
they are waiting for us to be seen

Such

right compels left
placidity instills steps
the freedom of waters resuming upward with as much grace as is flow
absence requests gain
enjoyment most alluring to pain
same place where happenstance meets one and leaves what is to grow
behind
the riches in continuance go forth as a relishing of pride
hear in solitude there are
effectuations unscathed yet afar
my journey aforementioned in divinity
my course
my par

introspektd: the languishing for love

Sprout

a pitcher atop my head with a time release sensitivity
its capacity brimming by word
each code
every symbol
painting with douse lines and heavy structure
yet fading into view
an elaborate pitcher atop my mind
with a brief like feel
cornerstone surreal
WHO GROWS THERE
it is eye who responds to the overseer
here to celebrate with my pitcher
TOUCHDOWN and GO FORTH
the crowd raves
a pitcher atop my head with a time release sensitivity
its capacity filled with words
that paint a dousing of soul

Grade

most gifts come wrapped and others just come
they are realized once the value seeps in and creates a leak of some sort
the policy calls it accidental discharge
then and only then can they find what the underwriter deems as cherish
the recipient takes a gratified loss
unwarranted as such...it remains a gift all the same
the saddest part about those gifts is they live for longest of times without ever having a name
embrace what if yours availed

introspektd: the languishing for love

Ride

an equestrian
that owns a dance choreographed on sole by pale moon
shadows and WINGS those interested the way
backing made of two steps and a locale posed as a new shoulder diagrammed to make plays
contemplated as
ever more left to go fishing to reach a nest where certainly
grows right-fully as rapidly as mold
looking to prove its presence in the era of novelty where its visitors relish in old
safe house
storage and facilitation whereas found a simmering on high
a longing, a sincerity and a gift that is absent yet mostly nigh

Ramble On

but
that
is
not
what
was
said

introspektd: the languishing for love

Utterance

when they come they are to endure their own strength
and go forth as discovery besides just be
transforming as they are
they must remember the power of their stance
they must go along with their own rhythm and resolve the village peoples dance
they must honor themselves as often as they are able
they must never return to void or their claim doubles unstable
they must strike the capsule of time moving preparation to complete
they must win the battle by creating a war for they know no one can compete
they must singular in omnipresence
they must take all that is necessary into account
they must be strong enough to carry but light enough to embrace that which will be let out
together in word

Hull

fiberglass
configured chastity that stores
only whatever further than one paddle can sing
upriver and back faced again leaving journey for the once and more
tides
waves
places that meet with regard to past brevity in me
eye recite a simple prayer awhile as ode to the elements
O how thankful I am to be

introspektd: the languishing for love

Grace

shielding honor
avail and tall
positioned for breastplates
determinable as it sends calls
withstanding at deck and corporal as it may
the very rise is in its succession
and most dependents are today
striking speed
and decorated unencumbered is definable yet
the epitome of life is accorded as my everlasting safety net

Cuff

the ever as glades
as sun fades
go under and rise again
stay wherever and near
the message frays send
whereas scuttled is fear
less than eye have ever known
Water
tooling and topical leaves all grown
where the sweetest of winds cover the solitary breeze
the essence of the natural seems always bring those willing to knees

introspektd: the languishing for love

Discount

your mind is a storehouse and I take of the goods there
my mind is open for business
I suppose we should share
take
take
make
shake the ritual before the seeds
currency of exchange sends forth the reality all needs
blessed blood on the cortex where treasure lay advance
sale on the music you make
it's time for the last dance.
count me in

Meet

this is my sword
laced in white and covered with chakra
is a boeing
bowing for honor that forces a stance of straight
for the scour
alas a heightened resemblance of a treaty within
my stake is the most heaviest lightweight that was ever to begin

introspektd: the languishing for love

Pact

"There are moments when the works of the past stare down at me with intensity. It is as if they have a brooding question and unable to ask it of me; as if they have forgotten that I have set them free."

Cadence

there laying underneath the ripple and somewhere in the midst
of the wave is a shadow
the shadow of the a reflection that has neared to come
its readying dependent upon the reaction to the reception

it is wading..wading in the mystery of all answers where there is
none other to be
except that which one who beholds chooses to accept

accept-dance
with this slowed speed, seek novelty in its space and face it as
if it were the last you could ever see
take flight in believing that the very ripple you are able to reflect
is the one that you were meant to be

introspektd: the languishing for love

Occupancy

Hold on to the moment but let it pass as it may
Hold on to what you believe or what you believe as evident by say
Remember that to hold is a most beautiful thing to do
Hold fast to your presence
Hold fast and onto you

Explanation

If I could describe this
if I could make due with this
if I could just be present to win
I would x-plane-to-u-a-nation
a nation of the embalmed elixir
a nation of you had better to be and love her mister
and deface the prides mask of individuality
and denounce thrones belonging only to me
I would do it for you
I would make sorts of adieu
one paddle remains in my canoe and it but a quiet stream
gazed worn but melodic the afro blue rhythmic section of the
last scene
it's angelic
you are angelic
going away and providing a dense
why i still do this to myself
even if 10 years ahead
will never really ever make sense

introspektd: the languishing for love

Geo-me-try

there is a searching that I have convinced myself of needing full attention
there is a putting off that I have convinced myself requires a bit; detention
there is a way and I seem to not acknowledge it for what it is
for the earth in me I try
there is a place that I go to in what appears solemn ways
there is a face that I wear departing
imparting both with last minute plays
no smiles just pale to match the mood of most
a fitting of the inn
then there is the air
most of which has turned to water-sinking and blazing both
for the earth in me i abide
I take here and i take now but what is there to leave for the essence of thee
what kind of fruit will these roots bare if were never to see
for the earth in me I still try
I coincide
I deny
and then after all I humidify
keep watch of the power of fire and water and yell STEAM
grey lines on blue canvas
a pass given by my evening sun
for the earth in me trying I must embrace spectacles of just THE one

introspektd: the languishing for love

Aggrandize

is there an answer for the call of loss
is there an essence for the home returned house
is there a worthy pause of time amidst still
is there one or another, a recourse for familiar

there is none
a maiden fair seemingly wished well
there is none
a voyage recapitulated
there is not ever one who is right with a void
of the emancipation of demise
its parlor of what was stoic

the celebration of the life

Gratitude

there are days where greatness seems to set in and aside. i take my attitude there.
there are other days where greatness tends and then subsides. i use my attitude as a plate.
there are times where greatness declines at the others' hands. i force my attitude to wait.
there are times where greatness is implication. i show my attitude to its fate.
there are seasons and reasons and joys untold where i greatly discover them. i move my attitude along so.
there are occurrences and opportunities and circumstances too bold. i go with my attitudes scarcity and allow the unfold.
there are times. these are times. it is always, fortunate or not, the right time to fuse greatness with attitude....GRATITUDE
may we all be so kind and with hearts' core.
tis not the holiday yall..its the SPIRIT

introspektd: the languishing for love

Gauge

there's a layering unfolded and wanting to meet the kindness of you
good sir and kind dr. please dress my wounds and leave your concerns adieu
like your staff and your rod and your inkling and bills
like your ability and your aptitude and your flavorful nights and midday frills
use the entire formality to keep in this gash of depth
hide it so that no one of a type see dangers and evidence of a another wept
change me
good sir and kind dr. unheard
make me your case and I'll attract a fame absurd
there is more trust here then a union over bridged
a kindness unfathomable but destined a midge
over and over, invoicing and again
I've acquired a new type cover up of a mess
it's unraveled and now realized your gauze not made of mesh
still waters

Math

the epiphany
do what you can
while you can
with whom you can and however you must but whatever you do
solve that which you will not regret

introspektd: the languishing for love

Fort

effort
the parts of me that try to preclude the parts of you
no one looks a way
we just go
effort
the times that I've asked thoughts be delayed
you just stood amidst and ignoring though your movement seemed slow
effort
for the fort
I'm ditching these strains
unloading dock and all
tossing the net with seagull grains
Moldy
told he UNBECOMING
maps untitled
water that couldn't reach
love that is unidentifiable on a contract of breech
characterizing what all needs said
placement over there but please not in my head
this can't be effort
this is otherwise

I-t-y

prosperity
adversity
both bred from severity
both assumed about dexterity
both existent in rarity
one repugnant
the other for a prize
one self-serving
the other at a demise
shall take both
or one over that other
reality is the child
absolute is the mother

introspektd: the languishing for love

Standard

facets and faces none of them make game

the rules are separately conjoined to empress-ship

it moves at its own speed

carrying the cargo

known precious has no name nor mane

facets and faces lay no claim to this gem

she is auspicious and proper

her delicacy unrivaled by past pains

she is the highest of tests

Fallow

to look
the allowance of find
the simple gesture of locating self
the continuance of adjust as in add just
regulate
accommodate
blow thru
abide under
asunder
halting another
the complex gesture of staying aware
inside a manner
outside the storehouse
in the midst of all of excavating
is a place called kept
stay there

introspektd: the languishing for love

Fibril

gather the garner
grip is completely withdrawn
balance is low
floods have come
and removed the hinges of pride and
bore down on the foundation of anything left behind
take the powder given
trees still survive
masquerade under the pragmatism
embellished by others
reflection
immense intrepid
choosing vehicles of speed that tend to slow
where it's distance goes and goes, puttering
faster than past far
state the men who are helpless of their own way
give to self
give to maintenance, deflecting dissection
give to the consummation of the ecology of flow
somatic time
somatic twine
so that you righteously let go
and gather for the garner as the grip is withdrawn and the word
proves to us that it is so

Rambling

its
not
fair
to
put
words
in
mouth
especially
ones
that
I
am
allergic
to

introspektd: the languishing for love

Inconspicuous

these tear stains turned ashes then some sort burned
these walls built not of plaster but of circumstance
position and force lands me this place
where
I'm forced to say things to you that I've found problematic to leave behind
your wait has become my malignancy
ability
to see us as anything other than its acquaint
the readying of me has forwarded all calls to faint
presence
essence
variance
unable to defy
time spent unjustly denying
what has occurred goes into a pot
and its withholding reminds us forgot
of what we have but have wasted in away
I wish these tears could go to the same place
and water a seed that desperately need grow
the crops we have been harvesting nood till and sow
our sun our sun our sun our sun
he
he and his magnitude are beyond words inept
the sacrifice of blood
Afterbirth
Flesh
soul of everything
can in all-ways be a moot point
in this leaving yesterday and then tomorrow's wings
then what brings such an indifferent bliss
I miss you then

Tarry

I got so much to carry
this purse with all its weight
this diaper bag across my breast plate
my coffee and my tea
and whatever sweet-
ener that's they all need
I got all this shit to carry
to come to the pass
as if that ain't enough
I gotta carry this big ole ass

introspektd: the languishing for love

Pawn

lukewarm is so much better
not hot for fear of boiling over
not cold for the tragedy of freezing and escaping life
in the middle
the middle is balance
all is well
if only there were other simpletons like myself

ponTIFical

everything is voice
either expressed or expelled

everything else is love
either lost, found, diluted, polluted, controlled, repressed, released or just plain and shapeless

and at the connecting of the two; the best

together become

remote

one writes, one sings, one hums a story unfolded

untold for it to be enriched and magnificent

glory in the story

everything is voice
either expressed or expelled

introspektd: the languishing for love

No More Rambling

that
is
exactly
what
I
said

introspektd: the languishing for love

Connect with me:

Facebook @Rachannis
Instagram @Rachannis
www.bytiffanyrachann.com